M000289592

"In these poems, the Eif
Florida, just as snow collecting on \
the same water flowing through the ~~~~~ ~~ ~
island off the coast of France collapses *here* with *there, now* with *then,*
interweaving Kercheval's family history (births, deaths, romances)
with the history of Paris (with all its light and music and subterranean
ossuaries). **No other living poet can quite equal Kercheval's
gift for blending melancholy and vivacity,** especially in the
handful of exultant, kaleidoscopic long poems that anchor this
stunning book."
　　　—Nick Lantz, author of *You, Beast*

　　　**"Paris, that magnificence, part luminaire, part
abattoir, Paris where Kercheval was born, is the setting and
subject of Jesse Lee's magnificent new book.** 'But it is madness,
you know, this trying to learn the truth about the past.' Here is her
effort and her poems, some in imitation of others—by Apollinaire,
Cendrars, Breton, Aragon and more. She writes for us these brilliant
facets of her life, and ours.' The door of my poem shop opens /
on the
boulevard. / Its display window / square cut diamonds of light.'"
　　　—Hilda Raz, author of *All Odd and Splendid*

　　　"*America that island off the coast of France* is a book of
searching and compassionate poems laced with the most robust
wit. You'll never look at Paris the same way again—or even this
world—when we see a city depicted as '*the* egg. / Wide or narrow,
it is a ribbon / of pastry, of moonlight, of butter.' **This jubilant
collection transforms and brilliantly guides us in love
and sorrows across the hemisphere and back again,** gently
reminding us, 'I am wearing skin not/ just clothes / Never mind the
wrinkles in both…'"
　　　—Aimee Nezhukumatathil, author of *Oceanic*

Previous winners of the Dorset Prize

Land of Fire by Mario Chard
Selected by Robert Pinsky

Almost Human by Thomas Centolella
Selected by Edward Hirsch

One Hundred Hungers by Lauren Camp
Selected by David Wojahn

The Well Speaks of Its Own Poison by Maggie Smith
Selected by Kimiko Hahn

Into Daylight by Jeffrey Harrison
Selected by Tom Sleigh

domina Un/blued by Ruth Ellen Kocher
Selected by Lynn Emanuel

After Urgency by Rusty Morrison
Selected by Jane Hirshfield

Severance Songs by Joshua Corey
Selected by Ilya Kaminsky

Archicembalo by G. C. Waldrep
Selected by C. D. Wright

Biogeography by Sandra Meek
Selected by the Tupelo Press Editors

Dismal Rock by Davis McCombs
Selected by Linda Gregerson

Dancing in Odessa by Ilya Kaminsky
Selected by Eleanor Wilner

Red Summer by Amaud Jamaul Johnson
Selected by Ray Gonzalez

Ice, Mouth, Song by Rachel Contreni Flynn
Selected by Stephen Dunn

America
that
island
off the
coast
of
France

>)(<

Jesse
Lee
Kercheval

Tupelo Press
North Adams, Massachusetts

Library of Congress Cataloging-in-Publication Data available upon request.
ISBN 978-1-946482-24-2

First paperback edition: September 2019.

Cover and text designed by Bill Kuch and composed in Palatino and Nutmeg.

Tupelo Press
P.O. Box 1767, North Adams, Massachusetts 01247
(413) 664–9611 / editor@tupelopress.org / www.tupelopress.org

Tupelo Press is an award-winning independent literary press that publishes
fine fiction, nonfiction, and poetry in books that are a joy to hold as well
as read. Tupelo Press is a registered 501(c)(3) nonprofit organization, and
we rely on public support to carry out our mission of publishing extraordi-
nary work that may be outside the realm of the large commercial publishers.
Financial donations are welcome and are tax deductible.

ART WORKS.
arts.gov

This project is supported in part by an award from the
National Endowment for the Arts.

For Dan

CONTENTS

ONE

The Red Balloon

I escaped America in a hot air balloon

the same way my great-grandmother
escaped the siege of Paris

I floated out of Florida
across the iron-gray Atlantic, headed for France
land where I was born

reading waves, stars, finally maps
looking for the lights
that signal Paris

until by morning
I was drifting past the *Tour Eiffel*, eye-high
safe enough

though a few Americans threw ice
fished from their cups
of Coca-Cola
The radio talked to me in French
the way it did when I was little
& I tried to understand

like a child
without thinking
without translation
without knowing words are spelled with letters
(but tell me — is that possible?)

is it possible to smooth a scar
to baby skin —

is leaving
ever painless? Is returning?

The City Where — *I'm Told* — My Mother Was Young

Long ago
the lens of a camera
uprooted
this city

from *Sacre Coeur* to the far suburbs,
pressed it between the heavy vellum of memory,
so to reach it is to cross a bridge
much longer, much steeper than the *Pont Neuf*.

In this paper Paris, my mother is a young girl
waiting for her lover by a stinking canal.
Or so I've been told by people who might
— or might not — lie to my face.

I pour over Atget's photographs
each street, each boulevard, each *arrondissement*
falling under his care,
falling into his camera and out of this world.

But photographs are illusions, devoid
of both *pot-au-feu* and the garbage
the cook leaves — though Atget photographed
laundries as well as bordellos.

I imagine my mother leaving me a message
by way of Atget. I close my eyes
and think I hear laughter
and telephones ringing — *but I'm wrong.*

I walk over the bridge Atget made
with his stiff little pictures
and find myself in the Gare du Nord.
all steam, white and gray

And my mother, *ma mère* —
is standing on the platform waiting.
She has always been waiting.
Unless — instead — she never did arrive.

Long ago
this city
uprooted

Triste, I imagine her saying, *so goddamn sad.*

God Over Paris

In the *toilette* at the top
of the Eiffel Tower, a *cabinet*,
a stall, in the men's room
costs 50 centimes but the urinals
are free, so my son, four,
stands next to his father
& for the first time in his life
pees standing up.

The line of men waiting to piss
is longer than for the elevator
or the bronze telescopes —
which charge 3 euros
to see Paris up close.
Something, it seems to me,
we just paid to escape.

How to explain this sudden desire
to urinate, to hold
your penis in your hand
at the very top of a tower
which, while too pointed to *be* a penis,
is — in its own iron way —
spectacularly endowed?

So like men, I think, to take joy
in the near impossible —
in flushing a urinal with water
that traveled 300 meters
straight up for the sole purpose
of carrying their urine,
triumphant, to the ground.

My son, leaving the warmth
of the men for the view,

looks at me with pity
knowing I lack the necessary equipment
to do what he has done
though just this morning, he saw
a gypsy woman peeing standing up

in the *Bois de Bologne,*
her feet spread, skirt hiked to her knees.
Her daughter called
to my son by name —
Had she heard me call him?
Had she read it in the stars?
Max, she said, *I'm thirsty.*
Give me a drink.

And though she spoke to him
in French, he understood
her need & gave her his warm Coca-Cola —
bottle shaped like a tower —
& she drank it
without stopping, like a diver
desperate for air.

Now at the top of the *Tour Eiffel,*
it is raining, fat drops
fall from the bruise-colored sky —
Max points to a cloud.
Is that God's butt? he asks.
Does He ever sit down?

The Pigeons of Paris

My children play teahouse
in a park hidden from
the wind by horse chestnuts
and architectural whimsy.
I sit huddled, watching pigeons
strut the sand around me,
their feathers oil-slick rainbows.
Paris pigeons, fat and thin
by lot. One with a single leg
hops along, the fattest still —
because people feed him out of pity?
Because he moves less
than the others with their relentless
restless bobbing?

Three blond *enfants* of Paris
appear, pushed in strollers
by African au pairs —
white skin cared for by dark —
like in my Southern childhood,
the same distrust and care.
One nanny has brought crusts
for the pigeons. The second shakes
her head. They are not pets,
she says, frowning. I like them
in pies, says the third. To eat bird
makes a man light on his feet.
I feel myself come unmoored,

rising from the circle
of this park, not on the effort
of wings, but floating
like a hot air balloon — Montgolfier
over Paris. The crowds, streets,
the restlessness fall away

until I am higher than the *Tour Eiffel* —
which in 1783 when Montgolfier flew
did not exist —
Paris below me a coal-fired cloud,
me as close to God
as man has ever been.
Still, all around me —
pigeons.

j'ai deux amours & one of them is paris

in the mother country of my mother where I happened to be born, illumi-
nated city east of everywhere I am, berth of all embarking, port of all re-
turn, street of truffles, bed of sharp remembered pain, on the banks, steep
banks, of the river seine — o paris, enigmatic antidote — o glove thrown
down which, *au bon chance*, climbs my hand again!

o paris, if I return to you, site of my commencement & — perhaps — my
cessation too, if I stand beside the seine, shore of my conception, whose
water smells, even to a sailor, like farmland ripe with *merde* — tell me,
paris, will this day be a reunion, a homecoming or a coming to? paris, I am
full of questions about my accidental birth. on this imaginary day, will you
answer me at last? "certainly, my pet," paris — or my long-lost mother —
says, "*regardez-vous!*"

so I do & see the sun slip behind the sugared dome of *sacre coeur*, put
the prickly sweetness in my pocket to munch for *déjeuner*, then stoop
to scrounge the trash as my mother was said to do & in the hush, I pick
weeds to use as flowers. in the calm, I find sticks to build a fire. in paris, I
do all this in paris, city I love as incurably, as irrevocably, as impossibly as I
happen to love my husband, a man who looks as sad as you.

Children of Paradise

Paris is an egg. It is *the* egg.
Wide or narrow, it is a ribbon
of pastry, of moonlight, of butter.
Paris is the light
gliding over our eyelids,
sneaking in even when we try
not to see. We know ourselves
through Paris & in this
Paris is as private
as blood & as public
as humiliation in high school. I broke a molar
on a piece of popcorn
watching *Les Enfants du Paradis*
in Paris, watching that luminous cloud Arletty
playing the heroine Garance.
Like the flower, she says
after giving her name. *What flower?* the audience
always murmurs. Me too —
& that's what I love —
the not knowing.
Just as no one in the Paris of the film
can truly know Garance.

But what with the cracked tooth,
watching this film about Paris in Paris
turned out not to be
the rush of paradise
I expected, but instead,
along with Baptise the mime,
I was in agony. Baptise
from his unconsummated love
for Garance. Me from my molar,
from the pain crashing through my nerves,
& for a moment I thought
ammonia & chlorine bleach

had come accidentally together
filling the whole theater
because I was crying,
because I couldn't breathe.

Then Paris
took me out of myself & into the souls
of the stars, filled me with great pity,
with a sense of infinite space as poignant actuality,
as the light from the projector
shone over the heads of the audience.
But there is more, much more
to Paris than that. In Paris, life
runs away, is a runaway
at play & passion is everywhere.
Paris dangles all possibilities before us,
clanging as loud as bells. The mind sees
as through a glass — *Heaven.*
The heart sees — as through a moving curtain —
worlds beyond the bones
of everyday.

Le Petit Hameau de La Reine

At Versailles, in this
toy hamlet,
Marie Antoinette,
Queen of France —
daughter of a queen,
granddaughter of a queen
mother of daughters
who would die princesses —
played at being
milkmaid.

In the same *petit hameau*
my daughter Magdalena
plays at being Queen —
her mother a professor
who wants to be a poet,
her grandmother a teacher
who wanted to be a doctor,
her great-grandmother a wife
who wanted to be loved —
Why do humans
have such unhappy
aspirations?

Around us, sheep decorate
the long meadows
of the hamlet — *sheep whose mothers were sheep,*
whose grandmothers were sheep,
whose great-grandmothers were sheep —
back into the wooly
mists of time. Sheep
who wish for nothing else,
ewes & lambs
who, unhurried,
crop the grass.

Life Considered as the
13 Locks of Le Canal Saint-Martin

Lock 1.

Okay, maybe not all lives —
but mine, born squalling
in a hospital two blocks
from the iron mouth
of the canal, that meeting
of nature — the Seine —
& artifice — the canal's first lock.
That meeting of nature —
my mother's useless labor —
& science — the surgeon's scalpel.

Sectioned, the doctors said
of my mother & years later
of me as well,
as if we were grapefruit,
crated cargo moving,
lock by lock, through the canal
to the linen-draped
tables of Paris.

But we were not fruit —
Mother & I —
we bled more like cattle,
like cows meeting their red fate
in the slaughterhouses of *La Villette,*
before descending the canal
as meat for the hungry
carnivores of Paris.

Lock 2.

Today, on this canal boat,

we are tourists
traveling the opposite direction,
Seine to *La Villette,*
in three slow hours, ascending
all thirteen locks —
the only people working
on this boat the sailor
who steers us
through each lock, casts
the tie rope, gathers the stamp
from the waiting
government official
& the tour guide,
his hands full
with a load of Polish grandmothers,
me — half-caste American —
& my two small, restless
children.
Ah, but *Le Canal Saint-Martin,*
is ready for us,
opening even for such a slight cargo,
though the Poles
& I — no longer young —
are meatier than the crew
or than my children
raised on cornflakes,
that dry American
invention.

  Lock 3.

We leave the third lock
& enter the tunnel that is the canal
in its early stretches.
Haussman — that perfect
expression of his Emperor's will —
covered the canal,

stinking as it was with commerce,
smelling too clearly
of what made Paris
all her money, to build
yet another grand boulevard.

He put the work of the city —
& its working class —
out of sight beneath the sidewalks
of the bourgeoisie. But
Haussman, Kind Dictator
of the New Paris, built skylights,
barred portholes, to let air
& light into the tunnel
& hid them in the parks
of his new, above-ground world.

Now green vines trail down
to meet us as we move
through the circles
of wavering sunlight
Haussman granted us.
Ghosts, my son Max says,
pointing at the reflections
cast upon the walls.
He is four & takes his theology
where he can find it.
Poor dead, Max says,
they didn't want to leave
their Paris.

In the gloom,
I see rats run along
the tunnel's narrow tow path,
their eyes as bright
as bits of sky in what seems
a day-long darkness.
I imagine being born

as both this dark &
this uncertain.
Not to mention
sickness, the soft sibilance
of death.

Lock 4.

But we do emerge & pass beneath
the Swing Bridge
of the Barn of the Beautiful
which stands above the lock
of the same amazing name,
the lock that raises us —
load of three Americans
& forty Poles — one step closer
both to sea level
& to God. In the sun,
we blink at horse chestnuts
in bloom & at pedestrians
who line the bridge above us —
one per step — as if posing
for a group photograph,
as if they were a choir
assembling to welcome us
to life or, at least,
to their forgotten piece
of Paris.

Lock 5.

Yesterday, in the lobby
of the *Hôtel Batignolles*,
my daughter Magdalena
sat on the floor playing
dreidel with a girl from Brooklyn

who asked her
if she had visited *Le Mémorial
des Martyrs de la Déportation,*
that splinter buried
in the tender tip
of the *Île de la Cité.*
I heard the girl speak
of the lights — numerous
beyond even a grown-up's
ability to count them —
that represent
the dead.

We had only climbed
the tower of *Notre-Dame*
& tried to count
the pigeons. No, Magdalena said,
setting loose the top.
But we saw the house
where God lived
when he was only little —
before we went wrong
& we killed him
anyway.

   Locks 6 & 7.

We pass the *Hôtel du Nord*
which was *"un film Marcel Carné"*
our guide informs us, starring
Arletty, famous one-named beauty,
who, when accused of having sex
with a German soldier,
replied: My heart is French
but my ass is international.
My son looks up
confused. To him an ass

is a wild horse from Africa
we visit at the zoo.

Sex is life, I learned from being
born in Paris &,
as every Parisian woman
knows, also a gamble
with both *la petite mort*
& death. Not to mention
the time Arletty spent in prison
for her collaboration.
But Max
is an American
& I'm careful what he hears.

We pass, too, *l'Hôpital Saint-Louis*,
built to care
for the plague victims of Paris,
that has a museum
of six hundred plaster casts
of sexual organs deformed
by syphilis & gonorrhea.
One fact, thank God,
for my young son's sake,
our guide does not
seem to know.

Locks 8 through 11.

Now, the locks begin to blur,
the slow swooshing rise
of water is how the years
flow by. The Polish
grandmothers begin to nod,
chin on cushioned chin,
until we reach
the Lock of the Dead —

which brings us all,
even the oldest, briskly
back to life. Our guide explains
this was the site

of the Gibbet of Montfaucon.
Mont for mount, a site
so high all Paris could see
who was executed here,
hung from sixteen ropes
on two levels
so the hangman
could drop thirty-two souls
into the next world at one time.
Even in death, our guide says,
the aristocrats were up on top
& so had the better
view of Paris.

Imagine, he whispers,
the ravens pecking the eyes
out of corpses left to hang for weeks.
In the foreground,
perhaps a pile of freshly
quartered pieces from the guilty executed
in the city center.

He smiles, waves
a hand. "Thinking
of having lunch?" he asks,
"Let me recommend
a restaurant."

Lock 12.

& really —
what do we eat

but death,
each death a way of living?

   Lock 13.

We rise like a cork
inside the thirteenth lock
& sail at last out of *Le Canal Saint-Martin* —
If this trip was birth
then we are born.
If death, then wherever
the dead go, we have,
at last,
arrived there —

in the basin
at *La Villette* — our destination —
which was once both
the slaughterhouse
of Paris & the busiest port
in all of France. Now
it is abattoir
turned pleasure park.

In the distance, my daughter spots
a carousel, a slide
shaped like a dragon.
I take my children's hands in mine
& we disembark —
headed, as we humans
nearly always are,
toward paradise,
toward the promise
of a garden.

TWO

49 Answers to 50 Questions

1

I was born in Fontainebleau, France, in 1956
or
I was born in Paris

In Fontainebleau where Emperor Napoleon
bade farewell to his Old Guard
saying, *Adieu my friends! Would*
I could press you to my heart

Or in Paris near the Canal Saint-Martin
where barges moved slowly toward *La Villette*
the biggest slaughterhouse in Europe

2

My mother was either:

a Calvinist from Kentucky
a major in the US Army
who liked cigarettes & bourbon
& only married when she was 40

or

a French housemaid
a Jewish orphan raised in a convent
who turned 19 the day
that I was born

3

Both of them are dead
Both them lived in dread
of God & war
& bad news in the night

So do I

4

By the window in this rental cottage
are four birdhouses
but they are inside, not outside
so birds can only window-shop
only dream of a life inside a home
inside a home

I often feel the same

5

Either I had two mothers
or none
Neither option biologically speaking
possible for mammals

6

"The Jews deported from France
left quietly"—

there was, of course
some weeping

7

On Bastille Day, every year
I set my prisoners free

8

A fellow soldier shot
my mother in WW II. He was
mad.
She was lonely.

That was one mother —

the other was on her knees
in a convent saying mass while
her parents were gassed in Poland

At least part of this
is something that I know

9

My greatest fear? That I am wasting
my life — though since you cannot
hoard time like pennies, I'm not sure
what I can do about it

10

In my dreams
I fly. In my dreams, I am
always outside, looking in.
In my dreams, I am
inside a house that is
inside a house
inside a house. Birdhouses?
Universes? Then someone
shoots me from the sky
& I wake up

11

If I could be in France, 1956,
being born — I would know
once & for all
who my mother was

Why can't I remember?

12

Why does it matter whose womb
I was lifted from
whose belly the surgeon cut
whose blood the nurses washed
from my downy head? Forget it
I tell myself, death closer to me
every second than being born

13

& my own children closer
to me than any
of my mothers. Thus we set
the past wrongs right

14

which include all my
unkindnesses to both
my mothers

15

& give thanks
even for gifts
that came beribboned
in our blood

16

like the joy
I felt seeing
my own children
lifted from me

17

I should mention
my poor papa — who slept with
both my mothers
but who worked hard
came home
& read to me each night

18

I still tell myself stories
to help me fall asleep —
& it is his voice I hear
inside my head
even when what he is telling me
are lies

19

It was simpler when
I thought I only had one mother

I was lonely when I only had the one

When my daughter was four —
in a preschool where all the other
children's parents were divorced
& remarried or lesbians —
she turned to me & asked

Where is my other mother?

20

I wish I had just one of mine
alive
to be a grandmother
to my children

21

This cottage where I'm sleeping
is like a birdhouse,
bare wooden slats form
an A above my head
Outside my window I hear
owls & stars

not sounds you hear in Paris

22

My mouth tastes like black coffee
stirred with a metal spoon

23

coffee black as the dreams
of the blind. No, I have
no way to know that —

black as the dreams
of my Kentucky mother
who used to scream *no no no*
at night

24
Once I took my children to
the top of the Eiffel Tower
where all Paris lay
spread at our feet
like a dream of a toy city

25
Once I was going to have
a second daughter
& name her Lily

26
I'd be lying if I said I
always told the truth. Sometimes
I just forget to. Sometimes I
don't remember
anymore

27
Where do you find a legless dog?
Exactly where you left him

That's a joke

When my daughter tells it,
it gets me every time

28
If you cut the wolf open
do you get your child
your mother
back again?

Or does that only work
for woodsmen who carry
freshly sharpened axes?

29

I am not sure why
I wanted to name a daughter
Lily — a waxy flower appropriate
for funerals. For *fleur-de-lis,* I guess
for France
for everything I left there
birth mother
birth language
then Lily was lost to me as well

30

Love is a house
& we are hungry birds
inside it

31

Just writing that makes
me angry — me the chick
waiting for the worm —
in spite of having
two damn mothers. Why
am I so hungry?

32

Anger
is what keeps this birdhouse
warm

33

My mother was a soldier
unless my mother was
a whore

34

A linguist told me once
human beings exist
to carry words
from one location to another
Language, the chicks inside the
birdhouse
Language, what lives on

35

I also have a deep fear
of memory loss — forgetting even
what I cannot say I know

36

I am amazed by all
the things my son remembers —
names of kings, dates of wars
Little by little I am letting him
take over History
as a family dinner table topic

37

except for the secrets
except for the things
he will never know

38

It is madness, you know
this trying to learn the truth about
the past
It is madness to think
there is truth

39

It is a grace to write a poem
& share my madness
with you, gentle reader

It is madness to think what
I write down & you read
is still a secret. But I beg you —
please, do not tell a soul

40
Can I trust you?

41
I miss Paris
I miss having two mothers, both of them alive,
each holding a hand
as we crossed the *Champs de Mars*

I don't think that ever happened

42
I do not want to see
another funeral

I do not want to read
another will

I do not want to die
until my children are
much much older

I do not want to be buried
anywhere at all

43
I was born
a different person
one of those God chose, then —
subsequently, historically —
forgot

44

In French, my last name sounds
like "heart of a knight"
but is Breton & means
"horse house" or plain old "barn"

The first name I carry now means
"God exists" though
I'm no proof

When I was born
in Hebrew my name
meant "lily"

45

Once & only once
I was born on the same day
in the same country
to two very different women
& I have two birth certificates
to prove it

Proof, if you needed it
that words on paper lie

46

Maybe the answer
is that there are two of me —
& I am the only one
who doesn't know

47

Never assume
a complicated answer
when there is one so simple:

my birth mother handing me
to another
never looking back

48

I want to go back in time
so I can hold their hands
so tightly
I get to keep both mothers

but I cannot

In 1956, in France, I was born twice
to two completely different mothers

49

I wish that were a lie

50

THREE

En Route to a New World

after Blaise Cendrars

The air in the plane is cold
the sea below the plane is gun metal
the sky above the plane is cold
my mouth tastes of gun metal
Goodbye Paris I am leaving you for good this time

Nothing about you means anything to me anymore than to the emigrants with me
        in Economy Class former citizens of the former Yugoslavia former
        Czechoslovakia former Soviet Union who are homesick for Paris too
        but cannot live there
I want to forget everything not speak your language anymore to go to bed
        in huge beds with soft piles of American pillows

& eat huge plates of food no one took any care cooking
& take long hot baths several times a day if I desire
& take baths in vast jacuzzis in new bathrooms in the company of more plumbing
        than anyone needs
& fall in love with that great tub full of scrubbing bubbles

Float on those bubbles
Become light as a bubble
Rise, float like a bubble
to the tip-top of being American
& live there

Tonight

after Pierre Reverdy

Life is as simple as a pencil
The moon is humming I can hear it
The cars on the beltline hum the same pitch
Tonight the headlights of cars illumine all roads
Tonight the streetlights in my head come on exactly at sunset
& the room I live in is going somewhere

Just one high beam is enough
Just one horn sounding
My joy is that car horn
My joy rattles the house
brings my neighbor
back from the long avenue that runs
only to the cemetery

I sing on key for once in my life
Laugh if you want
but it's true
my mouth opens & out come
notes popping everywhere flying into ears

Listen I am not crazy
sure I laugh running down the stairs
sure I laugh as I unlatch the screen door

In the moonlight
In the porch light
In the light of the beat cop's flashlight
I laugh because
you arrive right on time like
the mail never does
&

I open my arms to you

Union

after André Breton

My husband whose hair is eiderdown feathering cliff nests
whose thoughts are galaxies revolving farther farther away
whose waist is the trunk of an aspen
whose waist is the waist of cricket singing not seeing the wasp
whose mouth is a tulip frozen in May snow
whose teeth leave prints like the tracks of mice over that snow
whose tongue is made of daguerreotypes & ornithopters
whose tongue is made of clear gin
the tongue of a mannequin whose eyes never shut
whose tongue is a dream of a whisper of a kiss
My husband whose eyelashes are these words on the page
whose eyebrows are the bridge at Avignon, the land bridge from Asia
the half rainbow that never touches the earth
whose temples are the windows of a schoolhouse steamed by our breath
whose shoulders are tables set & ready for company
are shelves in the library full of books no one reads anymore but he loves
whose wrists are roots buckling the foundation
whose fingers are silver dollars pulled from my ear
whose *aisselles* are mere armpits
but are still where I nest like a house swallow on long summer nights
My husband whose arms are made of sea sand marooned on this vast inland plain
are a fusion of meat & the knife
whose legs are pistons in the brute movement
of steam engines & happiness
whose calves are strong as shiplap
whose legs are theolodites measuring the earth with each stride
are skeleton keys, are FBI agents under J. Edgar Hoover
My husband whose neck is *Sechssamttropfen*, those six velvet drops
whose throat contains the Valley of the Kings
& encounters in the bed of the ocean
where lives the fish who swallowed both Jonah & Geppetto's puppet
whose chest is the sea at night
is a Persian rug warming the marble floor of our imaginary palace

whose chest is haunted by the rhythm of ghosts breathing
of ghosts wanting what we have, wanting him back
whose belly is a curtain whipping in the moonlight
is a whirlpool in which all the world is drowned
My husband with the back of a river porpoise arched above the water
with a back of glove leather & silk aviator scarves
whose nape is satin conch shell & oyster on the tongue
& an iced tea glass slipping through sweating fingers even as I drink
My husband with thighs like an oak handrail polished by touch
with thighs feathered like shuttlecocks
gloriously & imperceptibly balanced
My husband with the sex of a forest mushroom, a horehound candy, a spyglass
an atlatl, a platypus
My husband with the sex of a diving pool
My husband with eyes mirrored with tears
with eyes that are black ice & magnetic compasses
with eyes full of arctic ocean
with eyes full of melt water to drink in the desert
My husband with eyes that are rain forests burning
My husband with eyes that are equal parts fresh water
& salt — all my body needs for love in this life

In the half-light of a new century

after André Breton

the twilight is a red snapper
& in the tangerine grove
suns hang burning from the trees

because I am waiting for you

& if you come walk with me
no matter where
miracles will hurry to meet us

A chameleon will press his cool belly to my heart
turn first a sad tan
then a jade jealous green —

because he loves you too

I don't know why
but the earth is deeper than water
is a turtle finally shaking off its shell

I saw you evolve
from the salt sludge of the ocean
I was there

Wait, no, I wasn't

I was waiting here even then
& I was sad
the sky between the leaves hard as a horseshoe crab

I shut my eyes —
I am where you see me

Where are you?

For Dan, After a Party

You do not always know what I am thinking.
Last night in the chill spring air while I was
talking nonstop about the war & the President & how
he will be the ruin of
        us, it was love for you that set me
on fire.
        Isn't that the way of things? What I
want, I can't have. Not peace or love. Not
        even a kiss. In rooms
full of strangers, I think only of you. I put out my hand —
what can I touch that doesn't
        remind me of you? When the children come in
on Mother's Day with their tray of scones & coffee
& you trail after —
        where would I be without your love?
        The weather, they say, is turning
for the better & tomorrow will be unseasonably
warm.

Poem Loud Enough to Wake the Dead

after Louis Aragon

Let's kiss loudly the two of us let's kiss
& say this rude noise is what we loved
is what we loved the two of us
Yes because this poem the two of us kissing
is rock & roll punk grunge is our beloved dead on the radio
I want to hear the blood in our hearts slamming
between us like feedback like reverb trapped
in a boarded-up record store in Hamburg Memphis Detroit
Hear our mouths fill with that thunder
Yes let's kiss like one of those drum sets
our parents never let us play not even in the basement
Yes let's kiss the two of us in Wembley Stadium
where history was made
in Nuremberg where it was erased
smeared across a blood-soused page
Yes because something must make noise sometime
Some thing Some one
or there is no history

Let's bang lips together
become the two of us a sobbing accordion a squeeze box
our pressed lips the gag that keeps
us from shrieking our bloody lungs out
Let's kiss buzz bombs falling on London sonic booms scud missiles
Kiss that's an order!
Then stop to listen in the stadium where the wind
howls over what we loved
what we've lost
One of them a century soon to be completely forgotten
the other a President waving then not waving
two fathers three mothers a brother a sister between us
One child Dogs pure & mixed Grandparents
houses & the things that lived in them

avocado kitchen appliances
clocks with Winchester chimes
the warm lips of our mothers & fathers
Who will remember if not us? Who
will remember us if not us?
The trail of your footprints in the sand I remember
on the sand by the Gulf of Mexico I remember
I remember your sunburned shoulder
I remember your sunburned lips sunburned feet
I remember a restaurant already half underwater
I remember your irises blue
as salt water the sad whites
red as the sun
all in the last half of the last century

My heart is a war the nation's already forgotten
My blood pumps to the slow beat of a military band
I was dead tired at my father's funeral
I want to be drunk at my own
Light fell Kodak blue on the cemetery grass
on the flag-draped caisson
I remember
tombstones like capped teeth
I remember
you
Time time time time
is the real violence

Time makes a joke of love
makes it a story no one bothers telling anymore
bloodless, ashen
You know your ashes
will be like your father's ashes
will be like the sand on the beach
where we walked
sand now underwater
now at the bottom of the Gulf
like the day we first slept together

is a square on a calendar in the deepest depth
of some county dump buried with Pampers
bloody tampons a Popeil's Pocket Fisherman
We slept together quietly for years
a pair of Pocket Fishermen
set it then forget it
until tonight
Kiss me like you mean it I say
make it smack

Yes, kiss me
with a record on the turntable
with the knob twisted to *Loud!*
Kiss me for
what we loved, who we loved
Kiss me now now now
now
on our unmade bed
on a pile of broken vinyl records
on our stars, such as they are
Kiss me for your bloodshot eyes
for the sun roaring in the sky
for eternity which is not silent but is screaming bloody murder
for your mouth which is not closed
for our love such as it was
& is
your lips on my lips
What a kiss!

Horizon

You ask me to imagine the arctic has come into my room
the white sand beach has disappeared
& frostbite clings to my fingers
The house is turning into an ice breaker
the sound of a iceberg calving has just reached me up here
In two days, we will arrive at the pole
Already we've passed the Florida–Canada border
I know there must be ice mountains & sheer cliffs ahead
but palm trees outside
hide the Northern lights behind sweeping green fans
Night falls drop by wet drop
I wait with you for hours

Give me that beer & the last cigarette
I am going back to Miami I am going to bed

Next Tuesday

after Robert Desnos

there will be a single moment
when I arrive at the exact middle of my life,
a fragment of a fraction of time more fleeting than a blink,
more sudden than satisfaction in bed

& I will be aware of that moment

stretching like a long road across fields of seed corn,
leading toward a distant tower where — if I could reach it —
my flesh would last forever, resist kisses, remain as untouched by the seasons
as the moon by the wind

Instead, there will be a jolt & a shudder as my husband's car starts up, shrieks
         into the night

& once again a drunk sings at the far end of the lake
& once again a feather drifts down on my empty bed
& once again my three clocks chime the same hour several minutes apart

& once again a passerby in the street turns after hearing someone call his
         name
except he wasn't the one I was calling

& once again after falling from the neighbor's tree
a marvelous apple rolls around in the gutter
only to be swept up by the streetcleaner

& once again my husband — already miles away — recalls a song,
long forgotten, & promptly forgets it again
while I am left to hum it, over & over

FOUR

16 poèmes élastiques: rubberbands around my heart

after Blaise Cendrars

1. Tower

Paris
I was eating an orange in front of the Orangerie

When suddenly —
it wasn't my birth
it wasn't a *Métro* strike
or the taxidermized animals
     in the Natural History Museum coming to life
or the Seine flooding, water whistling
     through the stacked bones in the Catacombs
or Jim Morrison rising in *Père Lachaise* whiskey bottle in hand

it was you
it was the *Tour Eiffel* it was sex

     O Tour Eiffel
I didn't give you my umbrella for nothing
I didn't leave my son's stroller in your elevator
to leave & never come back

I didn't write 2 novels with you on the cover
not to dream of you
when I sleep in a bed damp with sex

In Florida, palm trees are you
In Pennsylvania, rusting derricks
In Wisconsin, cell towers
In the Gulf, offshore oil platforms, blazing with light

the way fireworks, zodiac signs, arabesques exploded up your sides
in 1929

when you were the world's tallest
advertising sign CITROËN

You are my spine —
the one smashed to dust & then
made whole

You are my gallows —
if I am ever hung for
my crimes as I should be,
liar that I am, unfaithful daughter
of an unfaithful father

I have climbed other towers
I have eaten escargot in Windows on the World
on a table that — later —
fell burning
from the sky & took my waiters
with it

But you stand
But your elevators
still rise to the sky

Tower of towers, World Tour Tower
Paperweight, thermometer, desklamp
souvenir tower

I am, was born, hope to die in your
shadow

2. *Poémerie*

The door of my poem shop opens
on the boulevard
Its display windows
square-cut diamonds of light

Listen to the accordions
Listen to the *Bal Musette*
& know you have stepped outside time

The typewriters never heard anymore
in the world clatter here —
tat-clack-tat-a-tat
Everything black or white
but still burning burning

On the corner, workers
from the night shift drink
red wine at a zinc bar
as if this were 1956 & I
were just being born
bloody, squalling, by the *Canal Saint-Martin*

From time to time
a car passes through the *Arc de Triomphe*
on its way to great victory
or to commit an infamous crime

Today is film noir
Today is Belmondo
Today is France under the old new management

& my American father
drives a vast American car
with fins like sharks
down the *Champs-Élysées*
& takes his sleeping bastard child
from the arms of her French mother
who is walking, always walking, by that same canal

The mother who is France
who is the winter sale at *La Samaritaine*
the brakes squealing at the *Gare du Nord*
the old aerodrome that survived the war

a girl & a maid & a whore — maybe
though one raised by nuns

who might have raised me —
in this Marcel Carné film version of my life —
near the *Hôtel du Nord*
to no good end at all

& my life would have been —
a cigarette in the dark
a glass of *vin ordinaire*

short
dark
sad, maybe

but French

3. Portrait

I am asleep
I wake up
I write all this down
I write "Cathedral, possibly Notre Dame?"
I write "No such thing"
I write cow & you are one
I write knife &, by god, you are bleeding
        or I am
I write cock — because I want one
        inside me as much as my mother did

For France without sex
is my body without thighs
I write "ass"
& it's your ass
It's yours, reader
It's yours, lover

Who doesn't have one, after all?

Or I could be genteel &
       say the "ass" belongs to
       my fiancé, not to you

Just as I could say my mother
       was a milkmaid
       or a midwife
       not a woman with good tits, a nice ass

Or so I am guessing since my father slept with her
when he was married to someone else

Me, I was born thanks to a knife
the Eiffel Tower the corkscrew
looming overhead
Christ dying on the cross
in 1,000 nearby churches
even on the afternoon I was born
It gave me a taste for blood

Watch out —
I have ink left

I could cut your throat

4. Dance

Call me a wandering Jew
since my mother was one

No place for her in Paris
parents deported
she & her sister left at a convent
me, in turn, given away to a new life in a new land

But once sent on my way
I found I could not stop moving
continually coming & going
I became a woman who flies above
the world
gazes, disconnected, from a tiny window
at the blue or green or white below

Even the news doesn't interest me anymore
flicker/drone
Dance of disaster
Dance of daily deaths
intercut with the failed marriages
of those famous merely for being famous
But even those who fly
fall

One day, I will pirouette
Turn on one toe
Come down
from the clouds

If I die
If you die

I will smell it
the way I can smell
falling
snow

5. I Have A Body

I am wearing skin not
just clothes

Never mind the wrinkles in both
It is Glorious, this having flesh

Body wired with the most sophisticated sensors

My upraised palms are scales that weigh
the truth of everything

I can feel how much you want me
just by touching
my lips to the small of your back

O yes

Everyone else in line for the morning reveille
steps back, leaving you the lone volunteer
The sun undresses us
clothes fall to the floor
until we are only our skins
moving

Nothing in this universe ever stands still

Outside is the river
I can hear carp slapping, spawning
in the shallows

body on wet body

I love you too

6. Hammock

There is one on the porch
of this cabin on the Wisconsin River

There was one in the house
in Florida where I grew up

As a metaphor —
the hammock is not cotton or nylon net
but the curve of the earth
between where I stand & France

My future always my past

I sit today on a river that on early French maps
is spelled *Ouisconsin*

& read Apollinaire

Of whom Cendrars writes
"Apollinaire
1900–1911 for 12 years the only poet in France"

Apollinaire,
dead 92 years

& *voilà*

still, he lives

Am I that alive?

7. Siren

It is a song
It is static
Tour Eiffel as radio tower
television tower
cell tower

In René Clair's film
Paris Qui Dort the city is frozen
by a mad scientist's invisible ray —
every human paused, midstep,

like a stopped watch

Only the watchman at the top
of the Eiffel Tower
& the passengers on an aeroplane
just making a grassy landing
move in the morning sun

The silence total
except for the phonograph they steal
& take to the top of the tower
to dance in their equally stolen fur & pearls

The film moves
but the world below is
still
as a B & W photograph

A soundless world

Not like now — when the Spanish King
snaps at the President of Venezuela,
"¿Por qué no te callas?" Why don't you shut up?
& it echoes on YouTube
as downloaded ringtones
Shut up Shut up Shut up

Weather Underground promises
"A fair day for Paris"
but in this new century
I smell hellfire
I smell war

There is no future but the past

No, no scratch that
I am going to send this stripped chassis
of a poem on a long trip

by snail mail, by sea
to you in Uruguay

Let it be the future

Let it arrive —
infant Moses in a papyrus basket —
on the doorstep

of a new world

  8. Journal

Jesus
It's been decades since I thought of you —
not since I married then abandoned a husband
who was a Methodist minister
                    who saw you even in *Star Wars*
                    thought pop songs on the radio
                    were about loving you

Christ
My life has changed since then
except what hasn't. I am still the same
I wanted to become a writer
I still do

Here are the books I've published
shelves of them

For me, each one is about me
thinking about you

Jesus
what a life
shipwrecked, shell-shocked
Everything sunburned
skin splitting like an orange

My books hurt just looking at them
none the paradise, the peace treaty
I longed for them to be

Today, I spent a sad damp morning
thinking of dead friends
& writing in my journal
reading the *New York Times* online

Christ
the whole world ends up crucified
in the morning paper

arms spread, wings spread, spread eagle

You'd think another airplane was
falling from the sky
but it's you
it's me too

9. Midnight Express

The life I lead
is designed to keep me from suicide

Everyone else leaps
throws themselves under iron wheels
in a universe of ambulance sirens
& sad last calls in all the bars
on this planet

Get thee behind me, Satan!

I have an accordion!
I have music
when poetry leaves through

the screen door like a stray cat
like a lover who came for the night
without so much as a toothbrush

I have blood
microscopic bits of human tissue
under my fingernails from clinging
to the ones I love
when the tsunami tried to suck them —
time & again —
into the black salt
that is no earthly sea

But I don't know anymore. I don't
understand what you are saying —
Is that a poem? That last one?
Is that tiny thing
a camera & a phone?

I was born in a great city
rubbed raw by war
My son was born in a town
so quiet
I can hear my neighbors dreaming

He is 12 now & tall
How could he have ever come
first into
then out of my body?

If I told you the story
of human reproduction
& you weren't human —
you'd laugh

I no longer read books from libraries
dead Dewey Decimal world

This poem will be the last
I write with a pen

Bon Voyage, books I have written

See how you like
being alone — unloved —
in this world

10. At the Crossroads

4 houses sleeping
in the sun
an old dog, fur knotted like a bathmat

Dare to shout
Pirouette on toes
Movement color light
melting in my mouth
like chocolate

me, translucent
blazing
in the dusty street

Love, you said I
didn't know how to open
my eyes

But here I am —
blinded by the light

11. Bleu

Blue
only the sky over Paris
never the Seine
White

all the paper
the bureaucracy requires
even in this digital age
to decide if I am a citizen

Red
My mother's blood —
giving birth to me by cesarean
My grandmother pricking a finger
on a needle the morning
of her deportation —
the only blood she shed in France
which so neatly outsourced
the murder of its Jews

Red
coming to America
crying until my eyes
were swollen shut

White
the thin sheet of paper
declaring me
American

&
Blue
the color of my
American father's eyes —
my American mother's were hazel
but so sad
they looked blue too

12. *Les Vampires*

November 1915 found the walls of Paris
plastered with posters
of a woman's masked face
question marks wrapped around her

neck
like hangman's nooses
Qui? Quoi? Quand? Who? What? Where?

Les Vampires
Feuillade's silent serial
starring the great Musidora in skin-tight black
as Irma Vep — as thief & murderess —
her very name an anagram of vampire

Every turn of plot
really about death —
male actors disappearing from the serial
to die as soldiers in the trenches
Every plot twist
really about sex —
Every scene
really about desire —

Why else would Phillipe Guerande, crack reporter,
pull a tiny gun on Irma Vep
only to find she has stolen his bullets?

All he wants is Irma Vep
All we want is Irma Vep

To peel off her tight black body stocking
To be her when she stabs a banker
through the heart with her hat pin
& throws his body off the moving train

All Phillipe wants is
not to live with his mother
not to be the one too weak to be a soldier

For once
to be the one grabbing Irma Vep
around the neck in the Apache Dance

their breath, their tight hot chests
the bellows of the accordion

For once
to be naked with a naked Irma Vep

For once
for her to escape & take him with her

But all he gets for being good
is a single bed, night after night alone

In the final episode,
Irma Vep dies
a bullet in her heart

& leaves Phillipe to his life as a reporter

Better to have been stabbed by that hat pin
Better to have been thrown from the train
Better to have been gassed at the front like Apollinaire

Better to be a poet, liar, thief of words,
than a reporter —
16 million dead in WW I —
responsible, in the end,
for all the world's unpleasant
truth

13. A Life in Titles

Home Is France, 1956
Falling to the Sound of My Mother's Voice
We Step Quietly into the Future
I See God in the Movies
My Life is a Silent Movie
Things That Have Escaped Me

Grief in Paris
Last Poem
Bang

14. Rock n' Roll

has a Hall of Fame
& in it
Buddy Holly's high school diploma
a very skinny pair of Dylan's jeans

Never mind —
turn the radio on
turn the stereo up
let's go for a drive with the bass cranked
as far as it will go

Rock is the music of America
It is the best thing I have found here

I live in a town where Otis Redding's plane
plunged into a cold deep lake
& still the music plays

Take that, Edith Piaf!

In the next life, no pens only drumsticks
In the next life, sex, drugs & an electric guitar

15. Constructivism redux

Black & white & red
no need for other colors

I think about sex all the day
I think about you sometimes

I think about God more often
The earth is full of molten magma
The sky is full of snow

Everything — through my eyes — grows
dimmer, less in focus
even with trifocals

But
if the print is big enough
if the art is sharp enough

I feel the knife edge like the old days
Hear the breath of both humans & machines
Feel you trace a tongue along my spine

I gave birth the way my mother did —
split wide open

See me? Dressed in black like Irma Vep
Qui? Quoi? Quand? Who? What? Where?

Wet nurse for future poets
Engineer of student souls

See? In arabesques writ large
across
an accordion of sky

My portrait

16. *Every end has a beginning*

I have seen the Seine pushing hard
against its stone *quais*

but I am not there, not yet

I have walked along the *Canal Saint-Martin*
crossed a bridge, looked

into that oil-slick water
for a past unmarked by any stone

My passport says I'm still there

I have waited, bundled, on a platform
at the *Gare du Nord*

for a stranger to take me in her arms
Mother taking me from mother
Twice, I waited until they came to get me
Twice

then I decided to be born

not yet,
but soon

FIVE

On the Coast

after Guillaume Apollinaire

At the end, even I will grow tired of this wrinkled old world

Shepherdess O Ocean this morning your waves wash woolly gray sand

I am already fed up living with ideas that were new when
I was new & I feel ancient now

The last century my century recedes like a tide
that will never come back

Even monorails are antiques
Even space shuttles are old hat

In all Florida only the Ocean is never passé
the most modern up-to-date salt water in town
I am not the only one who is love-struck
wave upon wave upon wave upon wave
The sealed condo windows & the sea walls watch with envy
as a sign trailing behind a plane sings aloud to the sea
Here's poetry in the world that prefers prose
People, paperback mysteries filled with serial killers
Biographies of great men who made industries hum
by thinking they were as irresistible as the Ocean

I saw a pretty new condo this morning I forget the name
New & clean in the sun it was a bugle
Executives & exquisite executive assistants
drive from the condo Monday through Friday
to their offices but Saturday & Sunday they sit
in the sun while Mexicans water the grass
great trucks brought here to live too close
to the Ocean for anything so thirsty so tender
I love the swank of that condo

that didn't exist when I married
let alone when I was a girl

Here's the young beach & I'm still a baby
dressed by my mother in white only
I'm sunburned & with my big sister
Nothing is more fun
than peeling the skin off each other's backs
then burying each other in sand up to our newly pierced ears

It's nine o'clock the moonlight is low I leave my bed
My mother prays all night by hers
Meanwhile the ancient amethyst depth of the Ocean churns at my feet
forever
Behold the beautiful beach at Easter
Behold the inextinguishable moon at Easter
Behold my real mother
Behold my first love
Behold eternity
Behold the mirror of heaven that is heaven
Behold a god who does not die on Friday & rise on Sunday
Behold the lord who is deeper than any diver can fathom
who holds the world's record for both darkness & depth

I am walking on the sand alone inside a crowd
Seagulls & children scream come too close
but only the Ocean is touching me
Love sickness clutches me at the throat
Soon I will be far from the shore
Soon I will be landlocked living in Iowa
I feel the sea foam tickle my calf & think
I will never be loved again
If I lived in the Middle Ages I would enter a monastery
but I am not Catholic not even Christian
I never pray but overhear myself praying as I walk down the coast
sea shells listening like the ears of sisters buried in the sand
then the waves laugh & the laughter crackles like St. Elmo's fire
Sparks gild the sand beneath my feet

My life is a watercolor with a gold doubloon frame
My life is a window that looks on the Ocean
even when I am miles from the coast

Good-bye I was walking on the beach my thighs were bloodsoaked
It was & I have no wish to remember it was the death of beauty

Now I am on the shore of Lake Michigan
under arbor vitae trees bent from long winters
I am boating with friends
one from Pittsburgh one from Tennessee two from Wisconsin
none born near the Ocean
Among the lake weeds swim fish symbols of Jesus
I try to imagine how this water traveled from the Ocean
how I could possibly row or swim or float there I hear seagulls
& know there must be a way

I am sad near to death driving through Illinois
the only water the arcs of sprinklers raining on the parched corn
In traveling the clock runs backwards
& I go backwards also through a slow life
I go to the Ocean
at Christmas, vacation
I leave I return I leave I go back
The Ocean is moving closer to me also
but slowly by inches feet though maybe soon miles
Now I am on the beach on the Riviera
I am completely happy sand on my nose
& instead of getting on with my novel
I watch the shards of sea glass green in the sun

I am in France & the tide rises & falls fifty feet
so I am on the water
then not on the water
without moving from the café
The boats float sit in the mud rise toward heaven once again

Me in Miami beneath a mangrove tree

Me in California barking like a seal

Me in Venice on a water-taxi lost in the fog

Me in Amsterdam by a canal with a boy I will marry
who finds me prettier than I am
He's engaged to a girl from his high school
but we'll rent rooms near the Seine
I remember spending three days there & three in Avignon
where I learned how to stage-fight
with real swords so each blow rings blue steel
on a bridge that goes nowhere but into the water

Once I lived for a month on a barge
just to sleep in a bed moving over the water

I go on to more capricious dazed travels
just to be near water
I suffered from love at seventeen & again at thirty
I've lived like a lunatic I've wasted my time
I dare not look at the clock I want to weep all the time
Except on the coast
On the coast I love everything & am never frightened

On the beach from her dawn entourage of flames the Ocean
beams at me possesses me
my pain my insomnia
vanish always I am underwater

Now I am on the coast again it is Christmas
I am angry at the sight of so many hapless tourists
refugees even though I am one
We expect to find love in every inch of sand
& to return like kings to our abandoned houses
One family carries a red umbrella I carry my heart
their parasol & my dreams equally unreal

Some of the refugees retire to the coast as I long to
move into new condos Often I see them in the evening
as they take the air on their balconies
They walk the beach with legs as thin as sandpipers'
They are women mostly their men having died shoveling snow
frozen water dreaming of a tropical Ocean

This time I don't want to go north again ever
New Year's Eve I walk on the beach after a red tide & see fish
dying in rows on the sand facing the water
Looking at the Ocean lost to them forever
I don't want to go home to a creek or a pond or even a great lake
drink wretched beer where the wretched inlanders live
in a cavernous restaurant at night watching hockey on a big-screen TV

I want to live on the seam between the land & the Ocean

I want to lick my lips have my mouth taste of iodine

I walk all night alone when the high tide erases
everyone else's footprints
steals cigarettes beer cans floats spent fireworks lost wallets
all the human treasure

Alone when night impeccable night withdraws like the tide
I walk north along the coast past rows of dead fish
christs of uncertain hopes
christs who died for my numberless sins

Good-bye good-bye I say when the sun comes
knowing my suitcase is packed knowing I am already leaving

Good-bye good-bye

sun-throated sea

I take a drink of ocean water
It's my life I'm drinking

America

after Philippe Soupault

I do not dream America
I shoot bullets at the moon America
I am waiting America
I am counting the days America
Each night is a day America
Each night is my neighbor America
I hear each & every cry America
I see both the smoke rising & the fire America
I root along the highway like an armadillo America
I roll like a hoop snake down the Interstate America
Here is a city that is burning
Here is a city that is drowning
I've seen it before America
I am moving fast & the tide is rising America
there is heat & thunder & fear America
I am running America
I can't escape America
The clouds are empty of rain America
I turn my back America
I close my eyes America
I call out America
I cry out America
If I call all your names America
You America
will you come?

Acknowledgments

I would like to acknowledge with gratitude the magazines in which the following poems appeared:

Archipelago: "The Red Balloon"
Blackbird: "49 Answers to 50 Questions"
Crab Orchard Review: "In The City Where—*I'm Told*—My Mother Was Young"
Denver Quarterly: "Children of Paradise" and "En Route to a New World"
diode: "16 *poèmes élastiques*: rubberbands around my heart"
Field: "Le Petit Hameau de la Reine"
Hayden's Ferry Review: "God Over Paris"
The Malahat Review: "Life Considered as the 13 Locks of
   Le Canal Saint-Martin"
Margie: The American Journal of Poetry: "America"
New England Review: "Next Tuesday"
Prairie Schooner: "For Dan, After a Party," "Horizon," and "Union"
Quarterly West: "The Pigeons of Paris"
The Southern Review: "*j'ai deux amours* & one of them is paris"
   and "On the Coast"
Southern Poetry Review: "In the half-light of a new century," "Poem Loud
Enough to Wake the Dead," and "Tonight"

Recent and Selected Titles from Tupelo Press

Silver Road: Essays, Maps & Calligraphies (hybrid memoir), Kazim Ali

A Certain Roughness in Their Syntax (poems), Jorge Aulicino,
   translated by Judith Filc

Flight (poems), Chaun Ballard

Another English: Anglophone Poems from Around the World (anthology),
   edited by Catherine Barnett and Tiphanie Yanique

The Book of LIFE (poems), Joseph Campana

Fire Season (poems), Patrick Coleman

Epistle, Osprey (poems), Geri Doran

Calazaza's Delicious Dereliction (poems), Suzanne Dracius,
   translated by Nancy Naomi Carlson

Xeixa: Fourteen Catalan Poets (anthology), edited by Marlon Fick
   and Francisca Esteve

The Posthumous Affair (novel), James Friel

Leprosarium (poems), Lise Goett

Hazel (novel), David Huddle

Darktown Follies (poems), Amaud Jamaul Johnson

A God in the House: Poets Talk About Faith (interviews),
   edited by Ilya Kaminsky and Katherine Towler

Third Voice (poems), Ruth Ellen Kocher

At the Gate of All Wonder (novel), Kevin McIlvoy

Boat (poems), Christopher Merrill

Canto General: Song of the Americas (poems), Pablo Neruda,
   translated by Mariela Griffor and Jeffrey Levine

Ex-Voto (poems), Adélia Prado, translated by Ellen Doré Watson

Intimate: An American Family Photo Album (hybrid memoir), Paisley Rekdal

Thrill-Bent (novel), Jan Richman

Dirt Eaters (poems), Eliza Rotterman

Good Bones (poems), Maggie Smith

What Could Be Saved (stories and novellas), Gregory Spatz

Kill Class (poems), Nomi Stone

Swallowing the Sea (essays), Lee Upton

feast gently (poems), G.C. Waldrep

Legends of the Slow Explosion (essays), Baron Wormser

See our complete list at www.tupelopress.org

CPSIA information can be obtained
at www.ICGtesting.com
Printed in the USA
JSHW021210120819
1073JS00002B/5